Ghana-Togo Relatio   ue

-2000)

Abdul-Moomen Pantah

Ghana-Togo Relations Under Constitutional Democratic Rule (1993-2000)

LAP LAMBERT Academic Publishing

Imprint
Any brand names and product names mentioned in this book are subject to trademark, brand or patent protection and are trademarks or registered trademarks of their respective holders. The use of brand names, product names, common names, trade names, product descriptions etc. even without a particular marking in this work is in no way to be construed to mean that such names may be regarded as unrestricted in respect of trademark and brand protection legislation and could thus be used by anyone.

Cover image: www.ingimage.com

Publisher:
LAP LAMBERT Academic Publishing
is a trademark of
International Book Market Service Ltd., member of OmniScriptum Publishing Group
17 Meldrum Street, Beau Bassin 71504, Mauritius

Printed at: see last page
ISBN: 978-3-659-84909-1

Zugl. / Approved by: Legon,University of Ghana,Diss.,2002

CHAPTER ONE

1.1 BACKGROUND

Ghana was the first African country south of the Sahara to liberate itself from colonial domination. On 6th March, 1957, it gained independence from British colonial rule. In spite of its relative small size, its foreign policy was of tremendous influence the world over, particularly in Africa and the developing world. The broad tenets of Ghana's foreign policy relate to the promotion and protection of the sovereign interest of Ghana, the establishment of a just and equitable international economic, social and political order, the promotion of and respect for international law, and the adherence to the principles enshrined in the charter of the O.A.U. (now A.U.), the Commonwealth, Non-Aligned Movement, and other international organizations of which Ghana is a member.

Over the years, these tenets have been interpreted variously to suit the times and circumstances in which the country finds itself. Changes in political leadership, national priorities and regional as well as global developments are some of the factors that directly impact on Ghana's foreign policy direction. At independence, Ghana was best conditioned to develop itself and extend its support to other African countries still under colonialism.

The spirit of nationalism and the quest for a continental union of Africa found eloquent expression in Nkrumah's leadership and his policies towards the international community. In the years following independence, Ghana's foreign policy remained uncompromisingly anti-colonialist. Ghana also preserved its Pan-Africanist policy stance, which were woven into a pattern by Nkrumah and the Convention Peoples Party (C.P.P.) to form the main thrust of Ghana's foreign policy.

1

To this end, Ghana made frantic efforts to get the emerging new states to form a Union of African States (UAS) but with little success. The reason for this was the determination of the African leaders to jealously guard and preserve their sovereignty, newly won at independence. The persistence of Ghana and her allies to achieve this objective led to the division of Africa into two ideological camps namely, the Casablanca group and the Monrovia group. On the one hand, Ghana and some African countries which formed the Casablanca group, advocated the immediate and unconditional political union of the African continent to bring about its independence. On the other hand, the countries that formed the Monrovia group led by Nigeria, Liberia and Ethiopia, pushed for a gradual and systematic approach to Africa Unity and economic independence through functional cooperation.

The radical ideas of Nkrumah on the modus operandi of eradication of colonialism were inconsistent with the views of the Monrovia group most of whom were Ghana's neighbours in the West African sub-region, particularly, Togo, Cote d'Ivoire and Nigeria. Thus, cases of accusations and counter accusations started surfacing between Ghana and her neighbours. Relations between Ghana and her neighbours were further strained by territorial disputes, ethnic rivalries, incidents of border skirmishes, just to mention but a few.

Historically, culturally and in the field of economics, Ghana and Togo are very closely related. Apart from the fact that Ghana shares contiguous borders with Togo both in the Volta and Northern regions, the consanguine ties between them unite the peoples of the two countries. The point is that, the peoples of the southeastern part of Ghana (Volta Region) and the southwestern half of the Republic of Togo are Ewes. Similarly, the peoples of the northeastern part of Ghana and the northern part of Togo are, in the main, Konkonbas, Bassari and Bimobas.

The above notwithstanding, Ghana and Togo have had very chequered relations since independence. This was originally due to the Ewe unification movement and Nkrumah's quest to annex Trans Volta Togoland. The idea of adding Togo to Ghana was not only an anathema to Olympio[1], but also for him amounted to giving the sovereignty of Togo away on a silver platter.

However, Ghana-Togo relations later received a boost after the overthrow of Nkrumah in 1966. The NLC government abandoned all the radical policies of Nkrumah and made the policy of good neighbourliness its top priority. But subsequently, the relations changed as different governments came with different polices. For instance, the Aliens Compliance Order introduced by the Progress Party (PP) government, which culminated in the expulsion of foreigners in Ghana affected Ghana's relations with her neighbours.

These discords between Ghana and Togo, variously attributed to leadership styles, strategies for attaining national interest, ideological inclinations, among others, dovetailed into the era of the NDC government which, ruled Ghana from 7th January, 1993 to December 2000. Relations between the two countries during this period alternated between cordiality and hostility. The "chill and thaw" relations had on several occasions been coloured by accusations and counter accusations from both sides as well as mutual suspicion of actions of the other. In addition, acts of violence at times punctuated the cordial relations between them. Consequently, instead of cooperation, there had been discords between Ghana and Togo. Authorities of the two countries initiated moves to improve and sustain the relations. How this was done is what this study intends to find out.

1.2   STATEMENT OF PROBLEM

Under normal circumstances, Ghana and Togo should have the distinction of being the best neighbours in the West African sub-region. But from independence there has been a chill and thaw relationship between Ghana and Togo. Specifically, between 1992 and 2000, it became more profound. Was it a question of personality clash, a question of genuine security dilemma or a question of elite non-complementarity? The turn about of Ghana-Togo relations soon after 2000 makes it even more interesting to find answers to these questions. The problem is that the Rawlings era, especially from 1992 marked a very interesting point in Ghana's foreign policy. It was a time Ghana started ushering in constitutional rule and it was also a time when Togo was forced to go constitutional. Therefore it was a time that the foreign policies of two long reigning sovereigns in the West African sub-region came under the watchful eyes of their citizens and the international community.

The leaders of the two countries shared something in common as they had both changed from military regimes into constitutional rule. Also the fact that both countries are members of ECOWAS, should have made it imperative to ensure that measures were put in place to forestall any recriminations that would undermine ECOWAS. But why didn't they see issues from the same prism? A careful resolution of these questions would help in understanding the dynamics of Ghana-Togo relations within the period under study.

1.3   OBJECTIVES OF STUDY

The objectives of this study are to unravel the following:

1. The nature of the relationship that existed between the two countries under constitutional rule.

2. How leadership styles of the two countries influenced these relations.

3. To identify ways by which relations between the two nations could be normalized and sustained.

1.4   **HYPOTHESIS**

The study will be guided by the following hypothesis:

Political leadership, more than anything else, accounted for the chequered relations between Ghana and Togo under the NDC government.

1.5   **RATIONALE OF THE STUDY**

The policy of good neighbourliness is vitally necessary for countries that share contiguous borders with each other, especially at a time when regional and sub-regional integration has gained currency in international relations.

Apart from the fact that this work would contribute to the existing work done on Ghana's relations with her neighbours, it would also contribute to finding solutions to the dicey issues of the imperatives of a good neighbours policy for Ghana. It is hoped that the recommendations of this study will provide timely advice for policy makers and also provide a basis for further research into the area of international relations.

1.6   THEORETICAL FRAMEWORK

Even though various theoretical approaches have been used by different writers to explain inter state relations, we find the theory of realism most suitable for the purpose of this study. Realism is based on four main assumptions.

First, states are the principal and most important actors in the international system. In terms of its structure, the international system is anarchical with no central authority or power to regulate it. This assertion ties in well with the situation of Ghana and Togo within the period under study because both countries belong to international organisations such as the United Nations (UN), Organisation of African Unity (OAU) and the Economic Community of West African States (ECOWAS). However, not so much was done by these organizations to settle the Ghana-Togo impasse because of the fact that they do not have supra national powers. They are really a loose association of sovereign states and their effectiveness depends upon the extent to which member states are prepared to play according to the rules of these organizations.

Second, the state is viewed as a unitary actor. This means that countries face the outside world as an integrated unit and always have one policy at any given time on any particular issue.

Third, realists usually make the further assumption that the state is essentially a rational actor[2]. A rational foreign policy decision-making would include a statement of objectives, consideration of all feasible alternatives in terms of existing capabilities available to these objectives by the various alternatives under consideration, and the benefits and costs associated with each alternative. Thus Ghana or Togo, during the period under study, might have decided to close its side of the border after having done the cost and benefit analysis of such an action. One reason that Ghana preponderantly gave for closing its side of the border with Togo was the issue of smuggling and currency trafficking across the border, which subverted the Ghanaian economy. On the other hand, Togo has always advanced security reasons for closing its side of the border with Ghana.

Finally, realists assume that within the hierarchy of international issues, national security usually tops the list. In order to pursue this interest, the state has to increase its capabilities (military, political, and economic) in order to maintain its territorial integrity and sovereignty. This largely conforms to Morgenthau's position that, in a world in which sovereign nations vie for power, the foreign policies of all nations must consider survival the minimum goal of foreign policy. According to him, all nations are compelled to protect their physical, political and cultural identity against encroachment by other nations. Thus national interest is identified with national survival. Taken in isolation, the determination of its content in a concrete situation is relatively simple, for it encompasses the integrity of the nation's territory, of its political institutions and of its culture. As long as the world is divided into nations, Morgenthau asserted, the "national interest is indeed the last word in world politics"[3]. But a situation is created, where the security preparation of one state to preserve itself is perceived by others as a threat to their security. This creates a security dilemma for the states involved resulting in similar attempts by others to enhance their own security. For instance, Togo's preparation to protect itself against internal and external aggression in 1993, after foiling a coup attempt in which she accused Ghana of complicity, was interpreted by the Ghanaian authorities as preparation to attack Ghana. Hence the Government of Ghana announced that it had put the Ghana Armed Forces on a "third degree alert" – the first preparatory step of going into action and was considering calling Ghanaian soldiers on UN Peace Keeping operations owing to the situation in Togo.

The application of the concept of realism will therefore provide a good understanding of the nature of the relations that existed between Ghana and Togo under the NDC government.

1.7   LITERATURE REVIEW

1.7(a) GHANA-TOGO RELATIONS

A plethora of work exists on Ghana's relations with her neighbours. However, most of these works date back to the 1960s. Some of these studies would therefore be reviewed to serve as the foundation upon which this study is conducted. The all time most authoritative work on Ghana's foreign policy is by W. Scott Thompson[4]. According to Thompson, Ghana's relations with her close neighbours namely Togo, Cote d'Ivoire, Burkina Faso and Nigeria in the pre-independence and post-independence days were characterized by mistrust and suspicion. This was largely due to the radical and Pan-Africanist tendencies of Nkrumah and his desire to form a United States of Africa. To Thompson, Ghana's policy towards Togo between 1957 and the 1960s might be considered as a form of political irredentism. Using arguments drawn from the history of the Ewe-Unification Movement, and his own interpretation of Pan-Africanism, Nkrumah tried to frighten Olympio into surrendering Togo's sovereignty. The author opined that Olympio's refusal to succumb to the whims and caprices of Nkrumah resulted in bad blood between the two leaders, hence both accused each other of organizing subversive activities against their governments. It is however, important to note that, Thomson overemphasized on Pan-Africanism and political irredentism as being the bane of Ghana-Togo relations in the 1950s and 1960s to the neglect of other pertinent factors.

The thesis of Aluko's work largely conforms to that of Thompson. Aluko asserts that Ghana-Togo relations in the 1950s and late 1960s were strained. According to him, ideological and perceptual predispositions and political differences between Ghana and Togo created an atmosphere of mistrust, suspicion and fear, thereby enabling each of them to plan to subvert the other's government. He

8

concludes that the accusations and counter accusations that accentuated Ghana's relations with Togo during the 1960s, stood in the way of cooperation between them. However both Thompson's and Aluko's work are deficient in the sense that they did not cover the main thrust of this study. This is a void we intend to fill.

In his work, "The Ewe Unification Movement, a Political History", Amenumey[5] contends that Ghana-Togo relations were frozen especially after independence. Like Aluko, he believes that the strained relations were largely as a result of ideological divergence of the two leaders. According to Amenumey, this trend perhaps took roots from the Ewe-Unification question and Nkrumah's desire to annex Togo. To him, the ideas of Nkrumah and Olympio about the nature of the association of Ghana and Togo conflicted. He explains that, whereas Nkrumah rejected the idea of a federal structure and favoured a strong highly centralized government, Olympio favoured a loose association, preferably an economic and customs union. According to Amenumey, Nkrumah employed the argument of the Ewe-Unification but the fact was that, Ewe Unification never implied the loss of Togo's identity.

Youry Petchenkin[6] in his work "Ghana. - In Search of Stability", thinks that Ghana's relations with some African countries, especially those with pro-western regimes under the CPP government were becoming aggravated if not hostile. He believes that one reason for this discourse was the establishment of the Bureau for African affairs in Accra allegedly as a cover for military training of Africans in opposition to their governments. For him, this was a blatant violation of international law, which amounted to interference in the internal affairs of other countries, and explains Ghana's particularly acute clashes with Ivory Coast, Togo, and Nigeria.

Youry Petchenkin, however, thinks that Ghana's relations with other West African countries, especially after the Convention Peoples Party regime was not so strained. He contends that the National Liberation Council (NLC) reached mutual understandings with some countries that had market economies. In this regard, in April, 1967, a Conference on opening Ghana' borders with Togo, Burkina Faso and Ivory Coast (now Cote d'Ivoire) was held in Accra. According to Youry, negotiations were successful and in May-June, the borders were opened. The relations received a further boost when in June, 1969, Togo's Armed Forces Commander (now President) Etiene Eyadema paid a visit to Ghana. But the writer was forthright in stating that relations between Ghana and Togo from the CPP regime to the PNDC regime had never been even.

Asamoah[7], in his work, "Nkrumah's Foreign Policy 1951 – 1966" is of the conviction that in his determination to achieve African Unity in his life time, Nkrumah was impatient with others with dissimilar views. As a result of this, he assisted or dealt with opposition political groups in a number of countries, especially Togo, as to arouse allegations of subversion and interference in their internal affairs. According to Asamoah, by the time of the military coup of 1966 Nkrumah's influence in Africa was waning because of this and Ghana was suffering from some degree of isolation.

The work of Boafo-Arthur[8] in Ghana under PNDC Rule on "Ghana's external relations since December, 31 1981" complements the previous works, already noted. Boafo- Arthur believes that Ghana's relations with Togo during the PNDC days were rather troubled. According to him this was partly because of Rawling's initial radicalism and close alignment with Libya, which many countries in Africa accused of subversive activities. He further explains that the cordiality that hitherto existed between Ghana and Togo deteriorated after the coup of 31ˢᵗ December, 1981. This was because Togo was apprehensive of the spill over effect of the coup. The rise of Captain Thomas Sankara to power in Burkina Faso justified this assertion. His impolitic revelation that he had received military support from Ghana seemed to make the fears and suspicions of Togo genuine and Togo appeared to have strengthened her resolve to assist anti Rawlings elements.

1.7(b) **GHANA'S RELATIONS WITH HER CLOSE NEIGHBORS**

In discussing Ghana's relations with Nigeria, Thompson alluded to the assertion that Ghana from the very onset had very poor relations with Nigeria. To Thompson, this situation perhaps started even before Nigeria attained independence. He believes that there was suspicion and distrust between Nkrumah and some elites in Nigerian Liberation Struggle. Whereas Nnamdi Azikiwe and his National Council of Nigerian citizens (NCNC) found Ghana to be friendly and had cordial relations with her, it was the opposite with Chief Awolowo and his Action Group. Chief Awolowo found it difficult to come to terms with Ghana's leadership role given its small size relative to Nigeria. Ghana also had very uneasy relations with Cote d'Ivoire. According to Thompson, Houphouet-Boigny was very wary of Nkrumah's support of the Sanwi Nzima tribe to secede from Cote d'Ivoire. This manifested during the All African Peoples' Conference in Accra when Nkrumah refused to invite Houphouet Biogny because he regarded him as a "capitalist lackey of France". On the other hand, Houphouet rejected Nkrumah's socialist polices and accused Ghana of expansionist designs. This made cooperation between the two countries impossible.

In general, the contributions of the writers have brought out useful observations on Ghana's relations with her neighbours.

1.8   METHODS AND SOURCES OF DATA COLLECTION

This study relied on primary and secondary information. This included books, newspapers, journals, and magazines. It also utilized other materials of the Ghana Ministry of Foreign Affairs and open-ended interviews with officials of the Ministry of Foreign Affairs and Togo Embassy in Ghana.

The main sources of material or information were the Library of the Legon Center for International Affairs (LECIA), the Balme Library and Archives of the Ministry of Foreign Affairs.

1.9   ARRANGEMENT OF CHAPTERS

The study is divided into four chapters. Chapter one is basically introductory. It includes the background information about the problem, the statement of the problem, the objectives of the research, the hypothesis, and rationale of the study. It also includes the theoretical framework, the review of existing literature, methodology, and sources of data collection, the arrangement of chapters, and the limitations of the study.

Chapter Two looks at the national profiles of Ghana and Togo and a historical account of their relations from 1957 – 1992.

Chapter Three discusses the imperatives and dynamics of Ghana-Togo relations under the NDC government.

Chapter Four provides summary of findings, recommendations, and conclusions.

END NOTES

1.   Olympio was Prime Minster of Togo and later Togo's first President.

2.   Kauppi, M .V., and Vioti, P R., *International Relations Theory — Realism, Pluralism, Globalism*. (New York, Macmillan, Publishing company), pp. 6 – 7.

3.   Dougherty, E. J., & Pfalzgraff Jr L. R., *Contending Theories of International Relations, A Comprehensive Survey.* New York: (Harper Collins Publishers), p. 95.

4.   Thompson, W.S., *Ghana's Foreign Policy, 1957 – 1966. Diplomacy, Ideology and the New State* (Princeton: Princeton University Press, 1969), p. 308.

5.   Amenumey, D.E.K., *The Ewe Unification Movement: A Political History* (Ghana Universities Press, Accra, 1989), p. 338.

6.   Petchenkin, Y., *Ghana – In Search of Stability, 1957 – 1997.* West Port, Connecticut, London).

7.   Asamoah, O., "Nkrumah's Foreign Policy 1951 – 1966" in Arhin, K. (ed) *The Life and Works of Nkrumah* (Accra: SEDCO Publishing Ltd, 1991), p. 361.

8.   Boafo-Arthur, K., "Ghana's External Relations Since 31st December, 1981" in Gyima-Boadi, E. (ed) *Ghana Under PNDC RULE*. (Chippenhem: Antony Rowe Ltd, 1993), pp. 135 - 140.

CHAPTER TWO

NATIONAL PROFILES OF GHANA AND TOGO AND
RELATIONS PRIOR TO 1993

2.1   GHANA

2.2   HISTORY

At the end of the Second World War, nationalism became a major issue in most colonized states around the world.   In the Gold Coast, the surge for independence took shape quite early and nationalist leaders were forthright in the demand for independence.   In 1947, with the ban on political activities lifted by the colonial government, nationalist leaders formed the United Gold Coast Convention (UGCC) in the Gold Coast to fight colonial rule and to demand independence for the Gold Coast.

At the invitation of the UGCC, Kwame Nkrumah, then a student activist in Britain, travelled to the Gold Coast to take up an appointment as the General Secretary of the UGCC. Nkrumah's organizational prowess was incontestable and his rejection of colonialism was total and uncompromising.   These qualities in him, coupled with his ideological and tactical approach to the problem of colonialism was later to put him at odds with his colleagues who were rather elitist and conservative.

Increased nationalist activities in the Gold coast culminated in a countrywide boycott of European and Syrian merchandise and a riot in 1948. Nii Kwabena Bonni organized the boycott, in protest against exorbitant prices. It lasted for a month and spread throughout the country.   On the same day, the boycott was lifted, a demonstration intended to be peaceful was organised in Accra by some ex-servicemen. It was to present a petition to the Governor at his residence at Christianborg Castle. Police warnings for the crowd to disperse were ignored and so they opened fire, killing several people, including the leader of the demonstration, Sergeant Adjetey. This ignited a spontaneous rioting and looting throughout the country. In the end, 25 people were killed and 237 injured[1].

Even though the UGCC was not directly involved, its leadership was arrested and Nkrumah was severely blamed by his colleagues and made scape goat for all that happened. This precipitated his break with the UGCC to found a mass based party, the Convention People Party (CPP), in 1949 to spearhead the nationalist movement for independence. In its radical fashion, the CPP organized workers and farmers for the first time in a mass movement for independence and staged strikes and other actions. Nkrumah was imprisoned for "subversion and sedition".

Following this, the British Governor convened a committee of the elite, who drew up a new constitution in 1951, providing for internal self-rule and a legislative assembly that reserved large number of seats for chiefs and British officials. The CPP, however, won an overwhelming majority of seats in the 1951 elections, and British authorities released Nkrumah from prison to serve as Leader of Government Business and later, as Prime Minister. In 1954, Nkrumah's government introduced a new constitution that provided for direct elections by universal adult suffrage[2].

Nkrumah and the CPP faced stiff and intense internal opposition. The National Liberation Movement (NLM), led by Dr. K.A. Busia opposed the CPP in the 1954 elections. The NLM advocated the establishment of a federal state with regional governments, while the CPP pushed for a unitary state. Meanwhile, Ewe activists, concentrated in the southern part of British Togoland, strongly advocated unification with the Ewes of French Togo.

In a separate 1956 U.N. plebiscites however, majority of residents of British Togoland voted for unification with an independent Gold Coast and 70 per cent of voters in the rest of the Gold Coast territories voted for independence according to the CPP unitary platform. By that, the Gold Coast now renamed Ghana, was the first country south of the Sahara to attain impendence on March 6, 1957 from her colonial master, Britain, and was admitted into the United Nations Organization as the 82nd member in October, 1957[3].

2.3   GHANA AFTER INDEPENDENCE

As the first African country south of the Sahara to gain independence, Ghana became a model and inspiration for movements throughout the continent that were seeking an end to colonial rule. Dr. Kwame Nkrumah led Ghana to independence in 1957 and immediately proclaimed that Ghana's independence was meaningless unless it was linked to the total liberation of the African continent. To this end, he became the most outstanding African leader and the continent's most dynamic spokesman against imperialism, colonialism, and neo-colonialism. He ushered in a re-birth of the African personality and inspired the rest of the continent to gain independence.

Soon after independence, Nkrumah fashioned an economic policy, which sought to turn Ghana into an industrialised country. In this regard, he first sought partnership with private foreign capital. Later, he turned to state enterprises, import controls and credit management to spearhead his drive for industrialization and infrastructural expansion. Monumental developments took place and the Akosombo dam was built. Nkrumah built the Tema harbour and motorway, as well as the

16

Universities of Ghana, Cape Coast and Science and Technology. However, within the framework of otherwise enviable achievements, corruption and dictatorship blemished the Nkrumah regime. Nkrumah's extravagant expenditure on the continent depleted resources at home and in the midst of poverty and want, his "socialist boys" lived privately like lords even though they were supposed to propagate the ideals of socialism[4].

Nkrumah's move after independence to suppress the opposition heralded the beginning of his downfall. The Avoidance of Discrimination Act was passed in 1957. This banned all organizations, parties and societies, which were confined only to particular tribal and religious groups that were being used for political purposes. Consequently, the opposition parties merged to form the United Party (UP) led by Dr. K.A. Busia. In 1958, the Emergency Powers Act and the Preventive Detention Act (PDA) were passed. The PDA empowered the government to arrest and detain for five years anybody suspected of or found acting in a manner prejudicial to the defence of Ghana, to her relations with other sates and to state security. Furthermore, Nkrumah assumed increasingly autocratic powers and banned all opposition within his own party, the Convention Peoples' Party (CPP). In 1960, Nkrumah became head of government and state. In 1964, the government secured majority approval for a referendum that declared Ghana a dejure one party state under the CPP. With all avenues to constitutional change effectively outlawed, a joint military and police junta overthrew Nkrumah's government on February 24, 1966[5].

2.4   THE MILITARY INTERLUDE

In 1966, the stage was set for the first coup d'etat in Ghana. On February 24, the Ghana Armed Forces in collaboration with the Ghana Police Service overthrew

President Nkrumah while he was on the way to China on a peace mission to end the Vietnam War. The group was under the command of Colonel E.K. Kotoka with Major A.A. Afrifa. Two days after the military takeover on February 26 1966, a proclamation was issued establishing the National Liberation council (N.L.C.) which was to be responsible for the administration of the country. The NLC comprised 8 army and police officers with Lt.-Gen. J.A. Ankrah as Chairman and J.W.K. Harlley, Inspector General of Police, Vice-Chairman. The NLC suspended the constitution and ruled by decree. It also accused the fallen regime of corruption, suspended major development projects, released political detainees and proclaimed a market economy[5].

Three years later, the NLC created an assembly to draft a constitution for the return to civilian rule. In 1969, the NLC handed over power to a constitutionally elected government led by Dr. K.A. Busia. The Progress Party government virtually continued the policies of the NLC. A drop in the price of cocoa precipitated financial crisis in 1971. Against this background, the government raised prices and interest rates, cut spending and devalued the currency. This culminated in a wave of unrest and the subsequent removal of Prime Minister Busia from office on January 13, 1972 through another military adventure. The new military government, known as the National Redemption Council (NRC), and led by Colonel I.K. Acheampong excluded the leadership of the earlier NLC and reversed many of its policies. In 1975, the NRC was transformed into a Supreme Military Council (SMC). In the late 1970s, professionals and students held a series of nationwide strikes to demand an end to military rule. In view of this, the SMC agreed to a transition plan for the establishment of an elected government in 1977. But when the SMC allegedly rigged a referendum in 1978 approving continued military rule another wave of strikes moved the SMC to replace Acheampong with General Akuffo as the leader of SMC II

General Akuffo appointed a constitutional assembly and scheduled elections for 1979. However, to the chagrin and surprise of many Ghanaians, a group of junior army officers led by Ft. Lt. Jerry John Rawlings overthrew the Supreme Military Council (SMC) II and formed the Armed Forces Revolutionary Council (AFRC). However, elections took place as scheduled and after three months, the AFRC yielded power to an elected government of the Peoples National Party (PNP) headed by Dr. Hilla Limann. The PNP government gave way to the Provisional National Defence Council (PNDC) on December 31, 1981 in yet another military adventure, championed by Ft. Lt. Jerry John Rawlings. By the late 1980s, Rawlings started facing pressure from the international community to implement democratic reforms. The sequel of this was that in 1989, Rawlings promised to restore parliamentary democracy. The government announced a timetable for multiparty elections in 1992, and voters approved a new constitution. Rawlings' National Democratic Congress (NDC) won the elections with a landslide victory over the main opposition party, the New Patriotic Party (NPP).

2.5   GEOGRAPHICAL AND SOCIAL ATTRIBUTES

Ghana is a coastal country in West Africa that borders Togo to the east, Burkina Faso to the north, Cote'dIvoire to the west and Gulf of Guinea to the south.It has a total area of 233,537 square kilometres and its capital city is Accra. It is divided into 10 administrative regions and has a population of 18.4 million, (according to the 2000 population and housing census)[6].

Like most countries in Africa, Ghana has numerous linguistic, cultural and ethnic groups. Linguistically, the people of Ghana are composed of two principal sub-families. These are the Gur and Kwa groups of languages found to the north and south of the River Volta respectively. The Kwa group, to which most of the languages of the people of West Africa belong, is further divided into the Akan, the Ga-Adangbe and the Ewe sub-groups. To the area north of the Volta are the Gur languages. This group is sub-divided into three, namely, Gurma, Grusi and Mole-Dagbani[7]. The largest of these groups, the Mole-Dagbani, is further made up of the following peoples: Nanumba, Dagomba, Mamprusi, Wala, Builsa, Frafra, Talensi and Kusasi. Grusi is a general term used to describe a large cluster of closely related peoples who live in Burkina Faso and Northern Ghana. Among them are the Mo, the Sisala, the Kasena, the Vagala and the Tampolense. The Gurman, the third group consists of the Konkonba, the Moba or Bimoba and the Kyamba or Bassare[8]. English is the official language and the medium of instruction in schools. There are three main religions practiced in Ghana, namely; Christianity, Traditional religion and Islam.

Ghana has five principal vegetational zones. The largest portion, stretching from the north right down to the southeastern corner, consists of the Guinea Savannah Woodland that is predominantly open grassland area dotted with trees. Further, south is the thick rain forest. On the coast are two other very narrow belts, the coastal scrap and grassland strand and mangrove swamps of the southwest and south-east coastal stretches[9].

2.6   GOVERNMENT

Ghana is a constitutional democracy. The system of government is a blend of the Westminster parliamentary system and the United States presidential model. The Executive branch is headed by the President and assisted by a vice. The Legislative branch, a 200-seat parliament, is representative of the 200 constituencies in the country. A Chief Justice, who is appointed by the President, heads the Judiciary organ. It has the mandate to interpret the Constitution. The Supreme Court is the highest court of the land.

2.7   THE ECONOMY

The economy of Ghana is largely dependent on subsistence and commercial agriculture, industrial activities and bilateral and multilateral trade partners. Agriculture provides employment for about 55 per cent of the labour[10]. Gold mining, cocoa production, and timber lumbering are the principal sources of foreign exchange, although there are non-traditional exports such as banana, cassava, shea nuts and tuna. There is also a significant amount of manganese, diamonds and bauxite, which earn foreign exchange for the country.

Industry constitutes a substantial part of the Ghanaian economy. Mining, lumbering, aluminium production, and food processing are the main industrial activities. The primary imports are petroleum, consumer goods, foods, and capital equipment.

Ghana, to a very large extent, depends on foreign aid and loans to finance its budget deficits and undertake major development projects. Such loans and aid are solicited from bilateral and multilateral trading partners. The bilateral partners include the United States, United Kingdom, Japan, Germany, the Netherlands and Nigeria. International financial institutions like the Bretton Woods institutions, namely the World Bank and International Monetary Fund are Ghana's multilateral donor partners.

2.8   TOGO

2.9   HISTORY

The German protectorate of Togo was established in 1884, when the rulers of the region signed a treaty granting sovereignty to the Germans. From 1887 to 1889, Germany, Great Britain and France fixed the territorial limits of the protectorate. The Germans created the port of Lome and developed the resources of the region. In August, 1914, the first month of World War I, the Germans surrendered the region after an invasion by French and British forces[11].

In 1920, the final division of the area between the two countries took place, and Lome and the entire coastline were assigned to French-Togo in exchange for an enlarged British territory in the interior. In 1922, the League of Nations granted both nations mandates over their respective territories. On December 13, 1946, the United Nations (UN) granted France and Great Britain trusteeship over Togo to supersede the mandates established by the League of Nations. As a result of a plebiscite held in 1956, the British territory became part of the Gold Coast and was later incorporated into Ghana. In another UN supervised plebiscite in 1958, the National Union Party, which favoured complete independence, gained a majority of the votes in the French territory. Sylvanus Olympio, head of the party, became Premier. In February, 1960, Olympio rejected the suggestion advanced by Kwame Nkurmah of Ghana that the two countries be united. Togo achieved independence on April 27, 1960 and was admitted to the UN in September the same year[12].

2.10 THE MILITARY INTERLUDE

In January, 1963, Togo became the first country to experience military coup in sub-Saharan Africa. President Olympio of the National Union Party was assasinated[13]. The army selected Nicholas Grunizky to form a provisional government, and he subsequently assumed the office of President. In January 1967, the army staged another coup, installing Lieutenant Colonel Gnassingbe Eyadema, the army chief of staff, as head of government. The constitution was abrogated and the legislative body dissolved. In 1970, a plot to overthrow Eyadema was foiled.

President Eyadema promulgated a new constitution in December, 1979, under which he was almost unanimously re-elected to office being the sole candidate in Togo's first parliamentary polls since 1967. In January, 1980, the 13th anniversary of his coup, he proclaimed the Third Togolese Republic. In September, 1985, France sent troops to Togo to help suppress a coup attempt in which Ghana and Burkina Faso were implicated. President Eyadema was re-elected to another seven-year term in December 1986, but apparently bowed to popular pressure in August 1991 and yielded power to a transitional government, pending democratic elections. In subsequent months however, troops loyal to Eyadema repeatedly tried to overthrow the regime.

When elections finally took place in 1993, government sponsored violence and electoral manipulation led to the withdrawal of an international monitoring team and a boycott by opposition leaders. With turn out of about 36 per cent, Eyadema was re-elected to a five-year term. Parliamentary elections held in March 1998 were boycotted by opposition parties in Togo. The government's insistence on going ahead with June 21, 1998 Presidential elections, which Eyadema claimed to have won, attracted significant condemnation from the international community. President

Eyadema's current five year term of office ends in 2003 and he has given the assurance that the 1992 constitution will not be amended to extend his tenure to a third term[14].

2.11   GEOGRAPHICAL AND SOCIAL ATTRIBUTES

Togo, a small coastal West African country is located between Benin, Ghana and Burkina Faso. The population of Togo is estimated to be 5.1 million (2001 estimates) with about 37 ethnic groups. The largest of these are the Ewes in the south, the Mina and the Kabre in the north. About 70 percent of the population adhere to indigenous beliefs, while 20 and 10 percent are Christians and Muslims respectively. The climate of Togo is basically tropical in nature. The official language is French and Lome is the capital city.

2.12   GOVERNMENT

Togo after having been governed by a single party from 1979 to 1993 is now a multi-party democracy. The Executive branch is headed by a President and assisted by a Prime Minister, who is appointed by the President from among the majority party in the legislature. Legislative power is exercised by a unicameral National assembly with a total membership of 81 who serve five-years terms.

2.13   THE ECONOMY

Togo's economy is heavily dependent on both commercial and subsistence agriculture, which provides employment for about 65 percent of the labour force. Phosphate mining is the principal source of foreign exchange in Togo, though the economy is dominated by subsistence agriculture. Leading export crops are coffee, cotton and cocoa, which generate about 40 per cent of export earnings.

Togo is the world's fourth largest producer of phosphate and is by far the country's leading mineral product. Industrial activity is limited but growing. The leading manufactures include cement, palm oil, cotton textiles, beverages and soap. The principal imports are food and food products, textiles, machinery, electrical equipment, construction materials and transportation equipment. Togo's chief trading partners are Canada, Germany, the Netherlands, France, US, and Ghana.

2.14   GHANA-TO RELATIONS FROM 1957-1992

2.15   THE NKRUMAH REGIME

The strains in relations between Ghana and Togo date back to the pre-independence days. After 1918, following the defeat of Germany, the League of Nations divided the German Colony of Togland from North to South, a decision that divided the Ewe people among the Gold coast, British Togoland, and French Togoland.

After 1945, the United Nations (UN) took over the Togoland mandates. During the 1950s, when the independence of Ghana was in sight, demands grew for a separate Ewe state, an idea that Nkrumah, leader of the Gold coast independence movement opposed. Following a UN plebiscite in May 1956, in which a majority of the Ewe voted for union with Ghana, British Togoland became part of the Gold Coast[15]. After Ghana's independence in 1957, relations between the two countries deteriorated. Ghana was at odds with Togo over the Ewe-Unification question. Nkrumah placed a high price on the issue of re-unification of Ghana and Togo. His contemplation of a military invasion drove Togo into a defence entente with France though reluctantly. Differences between Nkrumah and Sylvanus Olympio, Togolese Prime Minister led to serious consequences. By 1959, both accused each other of plots and arrests were subsequently made. At that time, two opposition MPs were detained in Accra for alleged plotting, part of which took place on Togolese territory. Concurrently, there were reports of a plot against Olympio by Juvento, which had formally split from his party, and a section of which was in close touch with the CPP. The point is that both governments were becoming apprehensive about activities across their borders[16]. Nkrumah's objective was to ensure a complete union between Ghana and Togo. Realising that he was losing his chance of such a union, he offered dialogue and sent two officials in October 1956 to have talks with Olympio. An earlier move by Olympio for such a talk was put off by Nkrumah because Togo was still under colonial rule. This time round, it was Olympio who put Nkrumah off, claiming that Togo had to gain independence first.

From this time onwards, relations between the two countries aggravated. Nkrumah insisted on adding Togo to Ghana. His suspicion of France's intention in Togo made Nkrumah to order the army to conduct manoeuvres along the border with Togo. Nkrumah became convinced that Togo and France were up to some intrigues. Scott Thompson viewed this as a bad assessment of France's policy. Thompson may have gotten it all wrong in his assessment since Nkrumah's actions could easily and truly have provoked France to want to act as a parent that had just granted independence to one of its possessions. This is more so because of the military alliance that Togo had signed with France to ensure her protection against any possible invasion by Ghana. Olympio ridiculed Nkrumah for his (Boy-scout conception of military strategy) and referred to Nkurmah's bluff to make Togo the 7th region of Ghana the joke of the century[17].

Relations between the two countries were becoming complicated and by April, 1960, the problem was no longer a bilateral issue. The UN Secretary general, Dag Hammarskjold, intervened on behalf of Togo and urged Nkrumah to reconcile with Togo. Nkrumah visited Togo after Olympio refused his initial request to meet him at the Ghana-Togo border. The meeting did not seem to have patched up their differences. The tension escalated after July, 1962 assassination attempt on Nkrumah at Kulungugu in Northern Ghana. Nkrumah believed that his enemies were at work. A Ghanaian White Paper alleged that a massive plot against Ghana had been launched from Togo. The publication of the paper coincided with the date Olympio foiled an imminent coup plot in Togo December 1, 1961. According to statements from Togo, the principal in the plot, Christian Abbey confessed that he got his ammunition transferred to the Ghanaian Regional Commissioner's resident at Ho in the Volta Region of Ghana.

Nkrumah's intention of unifying Togo with Ghana was a situation Olympio could never agree with. The fact that there was bad blood between the two leaders prevented any compromise between them. Thus, when in 1963 the Togolese Premier was assassinated, there was wide spread suspicion that Ghana may have had a hand in it, and this weakened Nkrumah's prestige drastically throughout Africa. On the other hand, opponents of the Nkrumah regime were given moral and material aid from Togo until the overthrow of the regime on 24th February 1966. Ghana's relations with her immediate neighbours were so bad that when the CPP government was overthrown by the military, her borders with them were closed.

2.16 THE NATIONAL LIBERATION COUNCIL (NLC) AND PROGRESS PARTY (PP) REGIME

On the assumption of power after the February 24 coup in 1966, the NLC decided to change the situation. The NLC government denounced Nkrumah's policies towards the neighbouring countries, and made the cultivation of close relations with them its priority. Trade and other agreements were signed. To this end, in April 1967, a conference on opening Ghana's borders with neighbouring states was held in Accra. The participants included Togo, Ivory Coast and Burkina Faso. There was also exchange of visits between the Ghanaian Government representatives and those of Togo. In June, 1969, Togo's Armed Forces Commander, general Eyadema (later President), paid a visit to Ghana. The Progress Party government, which succeeded the NLC, virtually toed the line of NLC on foreign policy. However, Ghana's relations with her neighbours were marred by the Aliens Compliance Order in 1971[19].

2.17 NATIONAL REDEMPTION COUNCIL (NRC) REGIME

The National Redemption Council government of Colonel I.K. Acheampong that came to power on January 13, 1972 after the dismissal of the Busia government in a coup d'etat, quickly tried to repair the damage done by the Aliens Compliance Order. It condemned it as anti-African and promised to review it in order to restore cordial relations between Ghana and her neighbours. It consolidated and expanded the scope of cooperation with Togo. For instance, the Ghana-Togo Permanent Joint Commission for Cooperation was established under the NRC regime. The first session of the Commission at the experts level, took place in Accra from 29 - 31 May, 1972. The ministerial session was held in Lome, September 12 – 18, 1972. Similarly, the Ghana-Toto Border Redemarcation Commission was established in July, 1974 within the framework of the Ghana-Togo Joint Commission for Cooperation[20]. The governments of the Armed Forces Revolutionary Council (AFRC) and the Peoples National Party (PNP) were short-lived. Nevertheless, President Limann, demonstrated the PNP's government preparedness to continue the good neighbourliness policy of the NRC, by paying a visit to Togo, in 1980[21].

2.18 THE PROVISIONAL NATIONAL DEFENCE COUNCIL (PNDC)

In the early days of the Provisional National Defence Council (PNDC) government, Ghana-Togo relations were characterized by suspicion, apprehension, distrust, and antagonism. Both countries traded accusations at each other. During the early1980s, Togo was worried about the contagion effect of the December 31 Revolution. Togo's apprehension of the revolution was legitimate in view of certain utterances made by some members of the revolution. Chris Atim, a PNDC member, in January 1982, highlighted the possible spill over effects of events in Ghana to neighbouring countries when he said "nobody could stop the exportation of good ideas and practices from reaching people who yearn for a change"[22.] As if this was not enough, Ft. Lt. Jerry John Rawlings, the leader of the revolution, declared emphatically in November, 1983 that:.

> "We know that our revolutionary process threatens those
> institutions and countries whose systems are based on the
> exploitation of the common man. And we can understand
> scientifically why they will want to destroy us"[23]

Earlier in June 1983, groups opposed to the PNDC made a major attempt to overthrow it. Most of the rebels reportedly came from Togo. In August, 1985, Togo in turn accused Ghana of complicity in a series of bomb explosions in Lome, the Togolese capital. Property damaged was estimated at one billion CFA francs. However, the charge was denied by Ghana, while the Togolese opposition in exile

29

claimed that the bombing had been triggered by some supporters of General Eyadema[24].

This was followed by a sophisticated armed incursion into Togolese territory on September 23, 1986. According to the Togolese government, a "terrorist Commando Unit" crossed over the border from Ghana and tried to seize the military barracks in Lome and the national radio station. Thirteen persons including six of the alleged terrorist died in the fighting that ensued[25]. But by far the most critical issue had been the foiled coup attempt, which was blamed on Ghana in 1987. It took the intervention of the then O.A.U. Secretary General to diffuse the built-up resentment and tension on both sides[26]. Nevertheless, relations subsequently improved in 1991, leading to the reactivation of several bilateral agreements.

END NOTES

1.   Krafona, K., *The Pan African Movement, Ghana's Contribution.* (Accra: Advent Press, 1991), p. 17.

2.   Africana – *The Encyclopedia of the African and African America Experience*, (New York: Basic Civitas Books, 1999), p. 834.

3.   Thompson, W.S., *Ghana's Foreign Policy, 1957 – 1966. Diplomacy, Ideology and the New State*, (Princeton: Princeton University Press, 1969), p.11.

4.   Oquaye, M., *Politics in Ghana, 1972 – 1979.* (Accra: Tornado Publications, 1980), p. 2.

5.   Boahen, A., *Ghana: Evolution and Change in the Nineteenth and Twentieth Centuries*, (London: Longman Group Ltd, 1975), p. 191.

6.   Provisional report of 2000 Population and Housing Census by the Statistical Service Department, Accra.

8.   Boahen, op. cit. p. 7.

9.   ibid., p. 2.

10.   Dickson, K. & Benneh, G. A New Geography of Ghana (London: Longman, 1970), p. 5.

11.   A Brief on Ghana-Togo relations, Ministry of Foreign Affairs, Accra, 2000, O.A.U. Bureau.

12.   ibid,

13.   ibid,

14   ibid,

15   Thompson, op. cit.p 12.

16.   ibid, p. 84.

17.   ibid, p. 85.

18.   Aluko, O. *"Ghana's Foreign Policy"* in Olajide Aluko, *The Foreign Policies of African States,* (U.S.A, Hodder and Stoughton, 1979), p. 75.

19.   Petchenkin, Youry, *Ghana – In Search on Stability, 1957 – 1997,* (West Port, Connecticut, London).

20.   A Brief on Ghana-Togo relations, op.cit.

21.   Petchenkin, op.cit

22.   Boafo-Arthur, K. "Ghana's External Relations Since 31 December, 1981" in Gyima Boadi E. (ed) *Ghana Under PNDC RULE.* (Chippenhem: Antony Rowe Ltd, 1993), pp. 135 – 151.

23.   ibid. p. 135

24.   Uwechue, Ralph, (ed). *Africa Today* (London: Africa Books Ltd, 1996), p. 1511.

25.   ibid, p. 1511.

CHAPTER THREE

3.1   GHANA-TOGO RELATIONS (1993-2000)

With the demise of communism and the global demand for democracy, coupled with civil society activism, President Rawlings of Ghana and Gnassingbe Eyadema of Togo, two intransigent military dictators in West Africa, ushered their countries into democratic rule in 1993. Though the people of both countries share a common cultural, historical, linguistic and socio-economic affinity, modern day politics has brought artificial barriers between them.

Relations between the two countries at the governmental level from 1993 – 2000 were chequered. There were ups and downs, or freeze and thaw in their relations. Some clear signals of this situation had been border closures, mutual mistrust and suspicion and accusations and counter accusations about aiding dissidents and political opponents to subvert the governments of both countries. Language and political ideology had also contributed to barriers, although across the border, the people are the same. No doubt, at the level of ordinary people there was a daily influx of people across each side of their common border.

This state of affairs took roots at independence and dovetailed into the era of the National Democratic Congress (NDC) which ruled Ghana within the period under study. As already noted, both President Jerry John Rawlings of Ghana and President Gnassingbe Eyadema of Togo ushered their countries into constitutional rule in 1993, after a long period of military rule. Under constitutional rule, it was anticipated that the two countries would have buried the differences that characterised their relations under the military regimes in the interest of democracy and peace in the sub-region. However, Ghana-Togo relations were not spared the ups and downs within the period under study. This chapter therefore looks at the dynamics of Ghana-Togo relations from 1993 – 2000, within which period the two countries were ruled by Flt. Lt. Jerry John Rawlings and General Gnassingbe Eyadema respectively.

3.2   THE PERIOD OF MISUNDERSTANDING AND MISTRUST

Ghana-Togo relations at the beginning of 1993 were at their lowest ebb. This was partly because, the Ghana Government in the wake of political upheavals in Togo entreated President Eyadema to put in place a credible programme for the return to civilian rule. According to the Ghana Government, the adoption of Constitutional governance was the only condition that would create a situation under which Togolese could go about their normal duties without fear. This call by Ghana was necessitated by the gross violation of the human rights of ordinary Togolese and Ghanaians living in Togo as well as the influx of refugees into Ghana. For instance, on February 7, 1993, the Ghana Broadcasting Corporation (GBC) reported that between 80,000 and 90,000 Togolese had come into Ghana since the events of January 31, 1993. As a result of this, a temporary refugee camp was created at Klikor near Denu in the Volta Region[2].

The Ghana Government registered its protest against the situation in Togo with a strongly worded press release from the office of the President on 31st January, 1993. According to the statement, the Government of Ghana had put the Ghana Armed Forces on a "Third Degree Alert" – the first preparatory step to going into action owing to the situation in Togo. A statement from the office of the President said the government was also considering recalling some of Ghana's troops serving abroad in peace-keeping operations. It noted with astonishment that the Togolese President, Gnassingbe Eyadema continued to deny the involvement of soldiers loyal to him personally, in the perpetration of acts of gross violations of human rights of ordinary Togolese. The Ghana government had been concerned about the political and security situation in Togo for sometime, the statement said, and had therefore contacted a cross section of the Togolese people in order to be well informed. Most of the contacts had unfortunately confirmed the worst fears of the Ghana government[3], the statement concluded.

In response to the statement, President Eyadema accused the Ghana government of aiding Togolese Ewes in their bid to topple the government of Togo. Colonel Sanezo d'Almeida, a spokesman for the gendarmerie, the security service of Togo, accused President Rawlings of harbouring Togolese dissidents. He attributed all the troubles in Togo to Togolese Ewes and noted that they were using Ghana as a launching pad to attack Togo[4]. Colonel Sanezo said the Togolese government had not demonstrated any provocative attitude towards Ghana to warrant the Ghana Armed Forces being put on alert and cautioned Rawlings to "remove the log from his own eye". He also warned that Togo would face any invasion from any quarter and fight to the last person. Further, he claimed that General Eyadema was prepared to retire, but would not like to see Togo divided by people who were inward-looking and would breed tribalism in Togo and sell Togo to Ghana. Colonel Sanezo accused President Rawlings of wanting to annex Togo and said Togo would not tolerate any acts of subversion against it and would bomb the Akosombo Dam in Ghana if it had sufficient proof of Ghana's complicity of any acts of sabotage[5].

In another development, the Togolese authorities implicated Ghana in an alleged attack on the Inter-Arme Togolaise, Lome's principal military garrison, which is said to be responsible for President Eyadema's personal security. The assault, which occurred on the March 25, 1993, led to the death of Eyadema's personal Chief of Staff, General Mawulikplimi Amegi and his Armed Forces Deputy Chief of Staff, Colonel Kofi Tetteh. According to the Togolese authorities the attackers came from across the Ghanaian border to the west. But this was vigorously denied by the Ghanaian Minister of Foreign Affairs, Dr. Obed Asamoah in an interview with the British Broadcasting Corporation (BBC)[6].

At the beginning of 1994, relations between Ghana and Togo became worse. On January 6, a commando attack occurred in Lome, which was described by Togolese authorities as an attempt to overthrow the government of PresidentEyadema. The Togolese authorities again accused Ghana of direct or indirect involvement and arrested Ghana's Charge d'Affairs in Lome[7]. Togolese troops then bombarded a border post at Aflao, killing twelve Ghanaians in the process. Seven Ghanaian fishermen were also abducted by Togolese naval officers. The dead were alleged to be shoeshine boys working on the Togo side of the border. Unconfirmed reports had it that the 12 were lined up by Togolese troops and brutally shot. The killings were alleged to have been witnessed by officers of the Customs, Excise and Preventive Service (CEPS) of Ghana, who had to flee for cover as the troops pounded the Customs Post with mortar fire[8].

Responding to this, the Ghanaian authorities warned that any further Togolese aggression against Ghana would be met with a stern response. The Foreign Minister, Dr. Obed Asamoah stressed that Lome should not take as a sign of weakness Accra's non violent response to unprovoked attacks from across the border. The Foreign Ministry said in a statement that Ghana had no interest in the internal affairs of Togo and stressed that the problem in Togo stemmed from the refusal of the authorities there to create conditions for normal political activity by every section of the country's population.

Much as Ghana was concerned about its citizens in Togo, it never took kindly to the aggressions and accusations launched at her from Togo. This was best captured in the words of Dr. Obed Asamoah, when he was briefing journalists and diplomats in Accra. "If Ghana has so far refrained from responding to these extreme Togolese provocations, it is out of anxiety to save the lives of innocent civilians and to maintain international peace and security. There is however, a limit to what Ghana can tolerate, and Togo must take heed. Any deliberate and unprovoked aggression will be met with commensurate response"[9].

According to the Ghanaian authorities, their Togolese counterparts had never on a single occasion been able to adduce cogent and compelling evidence to substantiate their claims. They further argued that, the Togolese authorities were guilty of ritually accusing Ghana for fomenting trouble in Togo whenever there were political disturbances there. It is therefore plausible to argue that, the only thing Ghana could be accused of is her repeated appeal to Togo to create an atmosphere of peace and tranquillity, so as to enable the people to live their lives peacefully without fear. This is because Ghana on several occasions argued that the disturbances in Togo stemmed purely from internal causes and the only way this could be nipped in the bud was for Eyadema to set in motion democratic processes, which would permit all political elements to go about their activities without fear or intimidation. The true picture of the situation might have been that Togo was unjustifiably pursuing an aggressive line against Ghana. This assertion could find meaning in the words of Dr. Obed Asamoah: "to proceed from baseless acquisitions to what virtually amounts to a declaration of war betrays the motive behind Togolese accusations". He further noted that Ghana was in no way interested in subverting Togo with which she is bound with so many historical and ethnic links[10].

The government of Ghana believed that Togolese allegation of armed men coming in from Ghana is further flawed by the version of opposition groups in Togo. According to opposition sources from Togo, the January 6 attack, for which Ghana was accused, was unfounded. They explained that Togolese security went on a raid across the border to Aflao, rounded up and killed some men whose corpses they then proceeded to tender in evidence as the perpetrators of the alleged assassination attempt[11].

Be that as it may, it is glaring from the above that Ghana and Togo were at daggers drawn and their relations were tainted with hostility and mistrust. This might well be attributed to the divergent perception the elite of the two countries had about each other. Whereas Ghana thought that the political upheavals and blatant violation of the fundamental human rights of Togolese and the incarceration of innocent civilians did not augur well for democracy, peace and security in the sub-region, Togo viewed Ghana's stance as interference in the internal affairs of Togo. Much as the authorities in Togo wanted to embrace democracy, they did not see threats and attempts by the opposition to destabilise them as being proper. Besides, they viewed Ghana's interference as support for the opposition in Togo..

However, allegations of the Togolese authorities of armed men crossing from Ghana and Ghana's complicity in the events in Togo was somehow confirmed on October 22, 1994. Togolese security forces caught five heavily armed dissident commandos as they were getting set to blow up vital installations of phosphate mining in the southern locality of Kpeme. The leader of the group, Agbalo Kofi, a military deserter said they infiltrated Togo from Ghana. In a statement made at the Paramilitary Gendarmerie Camp in Lome, the commandos said they were recruited by a group of political exiles in Ghana. They claimed that their organization was led by a certain Logo Dossovi and that they were based in Agbozume in Ghana's Volta Region. The group further said that their original mission was to hijack a school bus carrying children of some "big men" in Lome and take them hostage in return for a ransom"[12]. Unlike the previous allegations, which Ghana has continually refuted, she was silent over this one. But to what extent the assistance to dissidents was a conscious policy of the NDC government to destabilize Eyadema's government would be difficult to say. Political refugees are often not invited into any country but they find their way there and international practice requires that they be given sanctuary. Once they are a source of friction between the receiving state and the state of their nationality and where there are conflicts of interest, they are useful tool for destabilization.

3.3   RAPPROACHEMENT AND COOPERATION

By mid November, 1994, the tempestuous relations between Ghana and Togo took a turn for the better. Ghana appointed an ambassador to Lome, after long years of the Ghanaian mission being run by a Charge d'Affairs. This was regarded as a major leap in Ghana-Togo relations as was observed by Radio Togo "A new chapter has been opened between our country and Ghana". Ghana was represented by Mr. Nelson Kojo Dumei, who presented his credentials to the Togolese President, Gnassingbe Eyadema, on November 16[13]. A communique issued after the ceremony said Togo considered the move as a new stage in the normalisation of Ghana-Togo relations. In a diplomatic fashion, President Eyadema promised to appoint an ambassador to Ghana as soon as possible.

It would be recalled that both countries had not exchanged ambassadors since 1982. This move was therefore considered as a remarkable milestone in the diplomatic relations of the two countries. In this vein, President Eyadema stressed the need for Ghana and Togo to reactivate the traditional bonds that had hitherto existed between the two countries. According to the communique, the Togolese President said: "one cannot choose one's neighbours. Rather God chooses them. This is why Ghana and Togo are bound to live together as the same citizens of the Economic Community of West African States". This statement was indeed reconciliatory and bore testimony to the fact that cracks had appeared in Ghana-Togo relations and needed to be patched up.

On the issue of security, which caused the main strain in relations between the two countries, President Eyadema said that Ghana and Togo definitely needed a true climate of peace to devote their energies and resources to development[14].

Ghana-Togo relations received a further boost when at the 17th ECOWAS Heads of State Summit in Abuja in 1994, Togo stretched a diplomatic hand of friendship to Ghana. In a move that surprised most ardent cynics, Togo supported the nomination of President Jerry John Rawlings for the post of ECOWAS Chairman, a post that eluded the Ghanaian head of State for 13 years[15]. This diplomatic gesture was obviously not lost on Ghana. Since then, both countries appeared to have shifted ground a little, though Togo still expressed anxiety about the presence of 300 military deserters and die-hard civilian commando militants in training camps in Ghana's Volta Region.

After this, a joint border periodic review committee was set up to help defuse tension along the borders. On the Togo side was Colonel Seyi Memene, Minister of State in charge of security. While on the Ghana side was colonel Prosper Ahadjie. But the main pivot towards rapprochement was Colonel Seyi Memene.

One time Inspector-General of Police, Colonel Memene, said to have matrimonial links with Ghana, had a soft spot for Ghana. In September, 1995, he successfully led a Togolese mediation team to broker peace between Ghana and Cote d'Ivoire. The two countries had been embroiled in a "football war" following spill over incidents of killings of Ghanaians in Abidjan after an African Club Championship football match between Asante Kotoko of Ghana and Asec Mimosa of La Cote d'Ivoire in 1994. Both countries were banned by the African Football Confederation (CAF) from further continental competitions. But Colonel Memene, then Chairman of the Togo Football Federation, and Vice-Preisent of CAF, successfully negotiated an accord, which brought Ghana and Cote d'Ivoire to play two friendly matches in Accra and Abidjan respectively, thereby breaking down the ice of hostility[16].

Since then, Ghana and Togo had cooperated on security and drug trafficking issues. In August, 1994, Bawa Oumarou Dabre, a key suspect in the killing of Togolese lawyer Kokou Laurent Agbemavo in Lome was extradited to Togo by the Ghanaian authorities. In a reciprocal gesture, two Ghanaian suspects, alleged to have killed two policemen in Vakpo along the Ghanaian border, were extradited to Ghana at the request of the Ghanaian authorities[17] on October 18, 1994. The Togolese authorities explained that the extradition was in conformity with the letter and spirit of the Quadripartite Agreement, signed between Togo, Ghana, Nigeria, and Benin. Under the agreement, the four countries committed themselves to mutual cooperation in security matters and areas of tracking down criminals, drug traffickers and illegal traders in contraband goods.

That aside, history was made when a high-powered Ghanaian delegation led by Dr. Mohammed Ibn Chambas, then Deputy Minister of Foreign Affairs[18], arrived in Togo on 27th October, 1994. The delegation carried a special message from the Ghanaian Head of State, Flt. Lt. Jerry John Rawlings to his Togolese counterpart, General Gnassingbe Eyadema. The visit was purported to solicit the support of Eyadema for a peace accord brokered by Ghana in Akosombo in September 1994 between the warring factions of Liberia. In a seemingly flattery and diplomatic gesture, Ibn Chambas described Eyadema as a doyen among Africa's Heads of State and expressed optimism that the peace accords would not fail, if Eyadema added his voice.

Another landmark towards rapprochement in Ghana-Togo relations was in 1995, when President Rawlings paid a one-day working visit to Togo on July 26. The visit to Togo necessitated the postponement by 24 hours of the 18th ECOWAS Summit that was due to take place in Accra. This gave rise to speculations that Rawlings was on desperate fence mending and damage repairs mission, early enough before the start of the Summit. Though no immediate official underlying reasons were given about the visit, a communique issued in the northern town of Lama Kara gave much-needed clues for reasons of the visit. The communique called on the neighbouring states to strictly respect the protocol of non-aggression treaty signed by ECOWAS member countries in 1978. Under the treaty, ECOWAS member states are not expected to give support to, or encourage subversion and acts of political hostilities against each other. Such reaffirmation did indicate that a period of thaw had set in Ghana-Togo relations. The communique also affirmed the commitment of both Ghana and Togo to comply with the Quadripartite Agreement, signed in 1984 between Ghana, Togo, Benin and Nigeria, which advocated the use of dialogue and consultations in the resolution of conflicts.

On the bilateral level, both countries stressed the need to reactivate the moribund Ghana-Togo joint Economic and Border Demarcation Commissions, which had ceased functioning, presumably due to existing bad blood. President Rawlings, who was accompanied by retired Captain Kojo Tsikata, the man most Togolese accused in the past of having a hand in all the plots against Eyadema, told the cheering crowd that his visit to Togo marked the beginning of a new chapter in Ghana-Togo relations. According to Rawlings, it was not enough to talk about the peace process in Liberia if Ghana and Togo, who are next door neighbours, do not do their home work and mend fences in order to promote the economic development of their people. Among other things, President Rawlings said "the time has come for us to do away with the frequent incidents and frictions among us to strengthen us before we can go out to help our neighbours".

It is apparent that the above affirmations provided the indicators that relations between the two countries were growing from bad to worse and needed urgent fence-mending before it could get out of hand. In fact, it was a frank admission of past failures to cement brotherly relations with Ghana's next door neighbour. As a sign of satisfaction, President Eyadema gave immediate instructions to Togo's new ambassador, Follivi Assiongbon to take up post in Accra[18]. Ironically, however, neither President Eyadema nor any official from Togo was present at the ECOWAS Summit held in Accra the next day.

3.4   THE ROLE OF DISSIDENTS IN GHANA-TOGO RELATIONS

One major variable in determining the pendulum of Ghana-Togo relations is the question of dissidents. As has already been said, both countries have since independence been suspicious of each other as a result of the activities of dissidents.

The situation was worsened during the PNDC/NDC regimes. Rawlings, since 1981 has been accused by Eyademaa of offering sanctuary to dissidents who aimed at toppling his government.

The presence of Gilchrist Olympio,[20] an exiled Togolese opposition leader and a sworn enemy of President Eyadema, who had assumed some prominence in Ghana, might have played a major role in the strained relations between Togo and Ghana during the NDC regime. He held a Ghanaian diplomatic passport and a state property, the Aboso Glass Factory was divested to him[21]. Olympio also had the opportunity in Ghana to use the press to launch attacks at President Eyadema. For instance, on September 25, 1997, he held a Press Conference in Accra and called for the overthrow of President Eyadema of Togo. He also asked for the intervention of the West African peace Monitoring Groups (ECOMOG) in Togo. Togo on the other hand, accused Ghana of harbouring her enemies and allowing them to use the Ghanaian Press to launch attacks on her[22].

However, in 1998, trends towards improved relations between Ghana and Togo continued. Ghana moved the Togolese Refugee Camp from Klikor in the Volta Region to Sanzule in the Western Region in reaction to the Togolese concern about alleged dissidents activities associated with the camp.[23] On May 12, 1998, the Togolese President in a gesture to sustain the improved relations paid a two-day state visit to Ghana. During this visit, the two countries in a joint communique reaffirmed their commitment to instituting mechanisms to minimize the mistrust and misunderstanding that have characterised their relations. As a first step, the two countries committed themselves to engage in direct contacts and frequent visits at the highest official levels. They also agreed to work together to ensure economic development of the two countries through increased trade[24].

44

On sub-regional issues, they called for peace in Sierra Leone and appealed to the International Community to intervene in Sierra Leone. They also expressed their support for ECOWAS and the socio-political and economic reforms that were taking place in the United Nations Organisation (UNO). At the end of the visit, President Eyadema expressed satisfaction for the warm reception and hospitality granted him and thanked Ghana on behalf of the people of Togo.

On his return to Togo, President Eyadema issued a press statement on 19th May, 1998. In the statement, he referred to Ghana and Togo as two brotherly nations bound by historical and cultural links. He appealed to the people of Togo not to do anything to destroy the peaceful atmosphere that has been created between Ghana and Togo as a result of efforts by him and his Ghanaian counterpart. He made reference to the visit of President Rawlings on July 26, 1995 to Togo and his visit to Ghana on 12 and 13 May, 1998 as demonstration of their willingness to cooperate in all fields of human endeavour. Eyadema also entreated the Togolese security to cooperate with their Ghanaian counterparts along the Ghana-Togo border so as to bring to book the perpetrators of crime along the border[25].

However, in June, 1998[26], Gilchrist Olympio organised a press conference in Accra to protest the results of the Togolese elections, which he contested and lost to Eyadema. In an editorial on the Press Conference, the Ghanaian "Daily Graphic" newspaper cautioned the government of Ghana to be careful not to draw Ghana into Togolese domestic politics. Ghana's Minister of Foreign Affairs, Mr. Victor Gbeho responded that Ghana did not err in allowing Olympio's press conference and that it would not threaten Ghana's relations with Togo. Meanwhile, a cross border shooting between the Togolese security and an armed dissident group on August 16, 1998, put the armies of the two countries in a state of alert that involved troops movement from

Ghana. It took a combined effort of the two countries to dispel any fear that Ghana was sponsoring an armed conflict against Togo.

There was a considerable thaw in the relations from this time onwards. The only incident that engaged the minds of observers of Ghana-Togo relations was on June 30, 1999 when two Togolese aircrafts violated Ghana's air space and landed in the Volta Region. In response to this, the Minister of Foreign Affairs, Mr. Victor Gbcho visited Lome to meet President Eyadema and his government officials. According to Togolese authorities, the pilots explained that, they did not know they were in Ghana's territory. However, they were later punished because they were not on duty and the Togolese government apologised for that incident[27].

On the eve of the 2000 elections in Ghana, the relations were on an even scale. However, the closure of the Ghana-Togo border by the Togolese authorities still puzzle the minds of so many Ghanaians.

3.5   THE BORDER QUESTION IN GHANA-TOGO RELATIONS

One of the major issues that has marred Ghana-Togo relations, both at the official level and the level of ordinary citizens, is the question of the disputed border between the two countries. Ghana borders Togo both in the Volta and Northern Regions of Ghana. However, the border has not been properly demarcated and there have been conflicts between the citizens of these areas, as a result. These border disputes are traceable to the early 1970s. A Ghana/Togo Border Redemarcation Commission was established in July, 1974 within the framework of the Ghana/Togo Joint Commission for Cooperation. The Commission was given three responsibilities. First, the reconnaissance and physical clearing and redemarcation of the border; second, the examination of all border incidents with a view to solving them and thirdly, the determination and payment of compensation in respect of properties destroyed in the process of the physical demarcation of the border[28]. The Commission worked for four years and focused its attention on "hot spots", ie. portions of the border, where lack of clear demarcation had created disputes among the local people. Some of such spots include Abdulai Karaa, Asukawkaw, Ashanti-Kpoeta and Hanyigba-Todzi areas. It also redemarcated 300 miles of the 400 miles of the common border in the southern sector. Just afterwards, the Togolese stopped co-operating with the Ghanaian team [29]. At Saboba, Cheriponi, Yendi and Bimbila in the northern region where Ghana borders Togo, there are equally border disputes. The border between Ghana and Togo at that end is not demarcated. A market, a school, and fertilizer depot have been built by the Togolese on the disputed land at Kpetabe[30].

After a long period of silence, the Ministers of Interior of the two countries undertook joint inspection of the border, following disputes over farmlands along parts of the border. A follow-up meeting was consequently held in 2000. The authorities of Ghana and Togo have recently, again indicated their desire to demarcate the border. It is hoped that the demarcation of the Ghana-Togo border will help minimize the political problems between the two countries.

END NOTES

1.   Files of Ministry of Foreign Affairs, Ghana-Togo Political Relations, Africa and O.A.U. Bureau.

2.   West Africa, 8-14 February, 1993, p. 207. Ghana cautioned Togo about gross violation of human rights in Togo in a Press release.

3.   ibid.

4.   ibid.

5.   ibid.

6.   West Africa, 5 – 11 April, 1993, p 545.

7.   West Africa, 17 – 23 January, 1994, p. 88.

8.   West Africa, 24 – 30 January, 1994, p. 129.

9.   West Africa, 13 February, 1994, p. 221.

10.   ibid.

11.   West Africa, 17 – 23 January, 1994.

12.   West Africa, 7 – 13 November, 1994.

13.   West Africa, 28 November – 4th December, 1994, p. 2036.

13.   ibid.

14.   West Africa, 23 – 29 January, 1995, p. 104.

15.   ibid.

16.   ibid.

17.   ibid.

18.   Ibn Chambas is now the Executive Secretary of ECOWAS.

19.   West Africa, 21 – 27 August, 1995, p. 1321.

20. Son of the slain Togolese President, Sylvanus Olympio, whom Eyadema was accused of assassinating. He is also the leader of Union de Forces du Changement, Togolese opposition party.

21. The Vanguard, 24 – 30 July,, 2002, Vol. 1 No. 17.

22. Interview with Mr. Djan Kla, Charge d'Affairs, Togo Embassy, Accra, and Mr. Kinsley Karimu, Deputy Director, O.A.U. Bureau, Ministry of Foreign Affairs, Accra.

23. Press Briefing by the Minister of Foreign Affairs, 14th April, 1998.

24. Daily Graphic, 13th May, 1998, p.1.

25. ibid. Files of Ministry of Foreign Affairs.

26. ibid. From the files of Ministry of Foreign Affairs, O.A.U. Bureau.

27. ibid. Files, Ministry of Foreign Affairs.

28. ibid.

29. West Africa, 7 – 13 February, 1994, p.214

30. ibid. From the files of Ministry of Foreign Affairs.

CHAPTER FOUR

SUMMARY, RECOMMENDATIONS AND CONCLUSION

This study examines the dynamics of Ghana-Togo relations between 1993 and 2000. The main task is to investigate the extent to which political leadership accounted for the type of relationship that existed between Ghana and Togo within the period under review. The objective was to find out generally, the nature of the relation that existed between the two countries under constitutional rule, how leadership styles of the two countries affected the relationship, and to identify ways by which the relations could be improved and sustained.

4.1   SUMMARY OF FINDINGS

The study's first finding is that, when the NDC government came to power in 1993, there was a sharp downturn in Ghana-Togo relations. The reasons for the strained relations during this period have been incompatibility of the leadership of the two countries. Ghana perceived Eyadema's regime as dictatorial and urged him to create a congenial democratic environment in which Togolese could live their normal lives without fear. On his part, Eyadema perceived the Ghanaian authorities as being opposed to his government and accused Ghana of complicity in all the political disturbances and coup attempts in Togo. Ghana however, denied these allegations and indicated that, it had no interest in destabilising the government of a country with which she shares strong cultural and historical ties.

It was found that there was no dialogue between Ghana and Togo at the height of this misunderstanding. The Joint Permanent Commission for Cooperation and joint

50

Border Redemarcation Commission were both dormant during this period and that probably explained why the relations were hostile.

The study also found that the presence of dissidents in Ghana played a significant role in the dismal relations between Ghana and Togo. The accommodation of Gilchrist Olympio by the government of Ghana and his access to the media, through which he lashed out at the Eyadema regime was unacceptable to Togo. Togo interpreted this as a conscious and deliberate attempt by Ghana to make the Eyadema regime unpopular.

In addition, the study revealed that, the long standing border dispute between Ghana and Togo was a contributory factor to the poor relations between the two countries. As stated earlier, the Joint Border Redemarcation Commission was dormant during this period and did not do enough to settle the border dispute. Consequently, there were incidents of border clashes between the citizens of Ghana and Togo, both in the Volta and Northern Regions of Ghana.

It was also established that relations between the two countries started to improve from November, 1994. Notable evidence of cordial ties were in the diplomatic realm. Precisely on November 16, 1994, Ghana's newly appointed ambassador to Togo presented his letters of credence to President Eyadema. This was seen as the beginning of a new chapter in the relations between the two countries. Shortly after that, Togo also appointed an ambassador to Ghana. The improvement in diplomatic relations between Ghana and Togo was also demonstrated at the multilateral level. At the 17th ECOWAS Heads of State Summit in Abuja, 1994, Togo supported the election of President Rawlings for the post of ECOWAS chairman.

The study further established that, in 1995, Togo and Ghana started exchanging visits at the highest official level. In what was described as a landmark in

Ghana-Togo relations, President Rawlings and his entourage were given a rousing welcome at Lama Kara in Togo on March 26, 1995. The two leaders, Rawlings and Eyadema, exchanged pleasantries and embraced each other for the first time. This was followed up with a visit by a high powered Ghanaian delegation, led by the then Deputy Minister of Foreign Affairs, Dr. Mohammed Ibn Chambas on October 27, 1995. The delegation carried a special message from President Rawlings to President Eyadema, and also solicited Eyadema's support for a peace accord brokered by Ghana at Akosombo between the warring factions of Liberia.

Furthermore, it was realised that the two states also cooperated on security issues and expressed their readiness to abide by the 1984 Quadripartite Agreement between Ghana, Togo, Benin, and Nigeria, in which they agreed to cooperate on matters relating to cross border crime and drug trafficking. They also agreed to abide by the 1998 ECOWAS protocol on non-interference in the internal affairs of member states and abstinence from assisting dissidents against each other.

The relations received a further boost, when Eyadema visited Ghana on May 12, 1998. On this occasion, the two leaders pledged their support for the peace process in the sub-region and promised to abide by all existing treaties and agreements between them.

However, these cordial relations were nearly marred, when Gilchrist Olympio held a press conference in June, 1998 to protest the result of elections he contested and lost to Eyadema. The Minister of Foreign Affairs, Mr. Victor Gbeho intervened and explained that Ghana did not err for allowing Olympio's Press Conference and that it will not affect the cordial relations between Ghana and Togo. Again, on August 16, 1998, a cross border shooting between the Togolese security and an armed dissident group put the armies of the two countries in a state of alert. But the authorities of the two countries were able to dispel the fears of people that Ghana was sponsoring on armed attack against Togo.

Another finding of the study is that, on the eve of the 2000 elections, the relations were almost even. However, the closure of the border by Togo on the day of elections in Ghana engaged the attention of so many Ghanaians and dashed the hopes they had on the rapprochement between Ghana and Togo. This assertion may be vindicated by the prediction of Professor Kofi Awonor[1] that, the NDC has no chance of returning to power so long as leaders like President Eyadema remain in power. According to Professor Awoonor, on the day of elections, December 7 2000, the Ghana/Togo border was closed by Togo, thus preventing traders and other people who wished to come to Ghana and exercise their franchise from doing so. This however, confirmed a long held belief that the NDC government had always brought in people from Togo to vote for it during the previous elections.

It is however interesting to note that, there is a new political leadership in Ghana, while Eyadema is still the President of Togo. The sharp turn about in Ghana-Togo relation upon the assumption of office by President Kufour has raised the hopes of many Ghanaians and other observers in the sub-region that a new chapter in Ghana-Togo relations is being written.

It should be recalled that, President Eyadema attended the inauguration of President Kufour on January 7, 2001. President Kufour reciprocated this visit by attending the 34th anniversary celebration of Eyadema's ascendancy to power during which the former was decorated with the Great Cross of Mono, the highest decoration of the Republic of Togo.

This move by President Kufuor attracted widespread criticisms and condemnation by a section of the Ghanaian public since President Kufour was honouring an invitation to an anniversary, which marked the overthrow of a constitutional government by the military.

However, the sentiments expressed by President Kufour on his visit to Togo on January 13, 2001, gave clues that he was not just in Togo to participate in the anniversary, but to help clear the old image of Ghana as a suspicious and malicious neighbour. An overwhelmed President Kufour told the Press that, he decided to make Togo his first official port of call barely six days after he had been sworn into office to show his gratitude to the Togolese people and President Eyadema for the wonderful expression of support and solidarity during his swearing-in ceremony in Accra. In his own words "I am barely one week into the presidency of Ghana and it is only right that the sister state of Togo should be the first state to host me[2]". On ECOWAS, President Kufour declared: "The ECOWAS treaty talked about the free movement of people and goods, unfortunately, it has not been so yet. In my time as President of Ghana, I am hoping that Ghana and Togo will come to realise that we are one"[3]. With regard to the past incidents of cross border attacks organised, by some Togolese dissident groups against the Togo government, President Kufour responded thus: "In my time, definitely from my side, nothing will be permitted to stand between the sister countries[4]".

Later in an address, the Prime Minister of Togo, Mr. Agbeyome Kodjo, explained that the award (Great Cross of Mono) was conferred on Kufuor to congratulate him on his election as President of Ghana and to inspire him to work towards stronger ties between the two countries[4]. On his part, the Minister for Foreign Affairs (Ghana), Mr. Hackman Owusu Agyeman explained that, the visit was not only to reciprocate President Eyadema's presence at President Kufuor's inauguration, but also to demonstrate the President's commitment to developing excellent ties with Togo.

From the above pronouncements made by the leadership of the two countries, one can claim with a reasonable degree of certainty that, under the NDC government, Ghana and Togo were ever apprehensive and suspicions of one another and that the cordial relationship that existed between them during the later days of the NDC regime was mere political rhetoric and for that matter superficial. On the other hand, the sharp improvement in Ghana-Togo relations under President Kufour and Eyadema, may well be understood in the assertion of Damarchi that,. "compatible development ideologies on the part of leaders contribute to cordial relations between nation-states"[6].

It is in the light of this that, it is hoped the recent measures will be interpreted in a good spirit, and that the bonds of genuine friendship, based on mutual trust and respect will be maintained and strengthened in the years to come.

4.2   RECOMMENDATIONS

In order to improve and sustain the good relations between Ghana and Togo, the leaders should have the political will to execute programmes. The political will to forge closer ties is the most crucial factor in sustaining cordial relations between countries. Without political will, all forms of cooperation in other fields may not be possible or at best be limited to political rhetoric.

Apart from the political will, which is the main determinant, the other areas that would help in improving and sustaining Ghana-Togo relations include:

a.   Democratic Consolidation - The consolidation of democracy in Ghana and Togo is a categorical imperative. This will ensure continuity in foreign policy objectives. Equally, it will enhance the image of the two countries among the comity of nations, thus keeping them in a better position to influence developments in the sub-region. Finally, and more importantly, democratic consolidation would help minimize, if not eradicate political disturbances and attempts by disgruntled elements to overthrow the government either in Ghana or Togo.

b.   Economic Cooperation – Increased economic cooperation between the two countries is paramount. The pattern of trade between Ghana and Togo over the last decade did not show significant trade relations. Trade between the two countries is virtually at the ordinary and unofficial level. The two countries should forge closer trade relations in order to enjoy the benefits of comparative cost advantage. There is a great deal of informal trade between the two countries. This situation should be exploited to further cement the cordial ties.

c.   Military Co-operation – Increased military cooperation is equally desirable. The steps already taken at "Operation Copienga 98"[7] and the celebration of President Eyadema's 34th anniversary, are well noted. This needs to be strengthened for it to materialise into Joint Military training, ship visits and exchange of cadets. The two states could sign a military pact so that in the event of external aggression on either of them, one could come to the other's aid. This would help nib in the bud, any tendency of the two countries going to war, even if there is tension between them.

d.   In the area of education, programmes should be drawn up by the two countries, which should include exchange of students, inter-university games and others. As a measure to solving the linguistic problem, the study of French should be made compulsory in Ghanaian schools as in the case of English with regard to Togo and other Francophone countries. This would be a further step towards the integration of the two countries.

e. As a result of ignorance of each other's laws there is the need to intensify political education. This would help conscientize the people about the laws of Ghana and Togo and prevent the situation where the law may be blatantly violated under the guise of ignorance.

f. In order to ensure closer social interaction, sportsmen and media practitioners, cultural groups, etc., should periodically participate in anniversary celebrations and national days.

g. There should be a frequent high level official visits between the two countries within the framework of the Ghana/Togo Joint Permanent Commission for cooperation. This would enable the two countries to discuss matters of common interest and act swiftly in the event of problems at both local and national levels. In addition to this, the Ghana/Togo Border Redemarcation Commission should be activised. The border redemarcation process should be fast-tracked in order to find a workable and lasting solution to the long standing border disputes between Ghana and Togo.

h. Equally important is the need to harmonize the customs and immigration laws of the two countries. In this way, the Custom and Immigration Services of the two countries could work in concert to check cross border crime.

i. The two countries should implement to the full, the ECOWAS Protocol on free movement of goods and persons.

4.3   CONCLUSION

It is clear from the findings that, political leadership, more than anything else, accounted for the chequered relationship between Ghana and Togo under the NDC government.

Clearly, the flux of domestic politics determines foreign policy objectives. Elite worldview within certain political contexts determine the kind of relations that may exist between nations. In both Ghana and Togo domestic politics was dictated by the whims of the respective elite. The ruling elite was held under the spell of strong hands - Rawlings in Ghana, and Eyadema in Togo. Their worldview and personal animosities towards each other dictated the trends in Ghana/Togo relations throughout the period under study. The thaw periods in relations show that other factors other than the personalities were at play. In the main, the dictates of democracy and international obligations forced some periods of thaw to be observed.

Democratic consolidation in both countries, especially in a post-Eyadema era, shall clearly improve Ghana/Togo relations.

In view of the fact that this study is by no means exhaustive, the need for more research in this area cannot be underestimated, and should be encouraged and pursued.

END NOTES

1. The Vanguard, 24 – 30 July, 2002, Vol. 1 No. 17.

2. Daily Graphic, Monday, January, 2001.

3. ibid.

4, ibid

5. ibid.

6. Damarchi, U.G., *Leadership, Ideology in Africa: Attitudes Towards Socio-Economic Development* (New York, Praeger Publishers Inc, 1976), p. 1.

7. A Joint Military Exercise by Ghana, Togo, Benin, and Nigeria.

BIBLIOGRAPHY

1. Aluko, O., "Ghana's Foreign Policies" in Olajide Aluko, *The Foreign Policy of African States,* (London, Hodder and Stoughton, 1979).

2. Amenumey, D.E.K., *The Ewe Unification Movement: A Political History*, (Accra: Ghana Universities Press, 1989).

3. Boahen, Adu., *Ghana: Evolution and Change in the Nineteenth and Twentieth Centuries,* (London: Longman Group Ltd., 1975)

4. Damarchi, *U.G., Leadership, Ideology in Africa: Altitudes Towards Socio-Economic Development* (New York, Praeger Publishers Inc.1976)

5. Dickson, K, Benneh, G. A *New Geography of Ghana* (London: Longman, 1970).

6. Dougherty & Pfalsgraff, *Contending Theories of International Relations, A Comprehensive Survey* (New York, Haper Collins Publishers 1990), 3rd Edition.

7. Kauppi, Mark V. and Viotti, Paul, R. *International Relations Theory-Realism, Pluralism, Globalism,* (New York, Macmillan Publishing company 1993) 2nd Edition.

8. Krafona, K., *The Pan African Movement, Ghana's Contribution* (Accra: Advent Press, 1991.

9. Oquaye, Mike., *Politics in Ghana, 1972-1979.* (Accra: Tornado Publications, 1980)

10. Petchenkin, Youry., *Ghana – In Search of Stability, 1957 – 1997.* (London, West Port, Connecticut 1998).

11. Thompson, W.S., *Ghana's Foreign Policy, 1957 – 1966, Diplomacy, Ideology and the New State* (Princeton: Princeton University Press, 1969).

12.   Uwechewe, Ralph, (ed) *Africa Today* (London: Africa Books Ltd., 1996).

Articles

1.   Asamoah, Obed., "Nkrumah's Foreign Policy" in Arhin, K., (ed). The Life and Works of Nkrumah (Accra: SADECO Publishing Ltd., 1991).

2.   Boafo-Arthur, K., "Ghana's External Relations Since 31 December, 1981" in Gyima-Boadi, E., (ed) Ghana Under PNDC RULE (Chippenham, Wittshire: Anthony Rowe Ltd, 1993).

Journals and News Papers

1.   West Africa, 5 – 11 April, 1993.

2.   West Africa, 8 – 14 February, 1993.

3.   West Africa, 17 – 23 January, 1994.

4.   West Africa, 24 – 30 January, 1994.

5.   West Africa, 7 – 13 February, 1994.

6.   West Africa, 7 – 13 November, 1994.

7.   West Africa, 28 November – 4 December, 1994.

8.   West Africa, 23 – 29 August, 1995.

9.   West Africa, 21 – 27 August, 1995.

10.   Daily Graphic, 13 May, 1998.

11.   Daily Graphic, 15 January, 2001.

12.   The Vanguard, 24 – 30 July, 2002.

Interviews

1.   Interview with Mr. Djan Kla, Charge d'Affairs, Togo Embassy, Accra.

2.   Interview with Mr. Kinsley Karimu, Deputy Director, O.A.U. Bureau, Ministry of Foreign Affairs, Accra.

Documents

1. Brief on Ghana-Togo Relations. (Accra, Africa/O.A.U. Bureau, Ministry of Foreign Affairs, 2001).

2. Press Briefing by Minister of Foreign Affairs on Ghana's Foreign Policy, Accra: Ministry of Foreign Affairs, April 14, 1998).

Table of Contents